THE COMPLETE ETCHINGS OF
REMBRANDT

THE COMPLETE ETCHINGS OF
REMBRANDT

EDITED BY BRUCE & SEENA HARRIS

INTRODUCTION BY FRANK GETLEIN

WITH AN APPRECIATION BY KEES VAN DONGEN

BOUNTY BOOKS A DIVISION OF CROWN PUBLISHERS, INC.

EDITORS' INTRODUCTION

REMBRANDT'S ETCHINGS stand as one of the milestones of Western culture. This collection is intended to place the full body of his work into as many hands as possible, because etchings and lithographs do represent the attempt of the artist to reach a mass audience.

The Introduction by Frank Getlein discusses the social impact of Rembrandt's work and the particular significance of his using the etching technique. The Foreword by the noted Dutch artist Van Dongen is particularly interesting for in it is a rare analysis of the inspiration and motivation of one artist by another. Obviously, Van Dongen identified with his famous countryman, and his romantic biography, while not scholarly or complete, offers a personal point of view which we found quite charming.

The essay was written in French and published originally in 1927. It appears here for the first time in English and was translated by George Lauscher. Van Dongen died in 1968.

The etchings are arranged according to the first comprehensive catalog made by Bartsch in 1797. The Bartsch catalog, prepared by subject matter rather than by date, lists twelve general groups:

SELF-PORTRAITS

OLD TESTAMENT SUBJECTS

NEW TESTAMENT SUBJECTS

PIOUS SUBJECTS

ALLEGORICAL AND HISTORICAL SUBJECTS

BEGGARS

EROTIC AND ACADEMIC SUBJECTS

LANDSCAPES

MEN'S PORTRAITS

MISCELLANEOUS MEN'S HEADS

PORTRAITS OF WOMEN

SKETCH PLATES

Some etchings, such as several self-portraits, appear out of these general categories, since Bartsch thought of them as general portraits. Later attributions have affixed the titles that appear below the pictures. Any numbers that do not appear in consecutive order are to be found among the rejected etchings at the end of this volume. These rejected etchings are arranged according to the original Bartsch numbers.

The dating process is risky; the dates provided beneath each picture are the result of scholarly consensus. The symbol (?) appears whenever two or more authorities were not in agreement.

For more exact information about chronology, we refer the reader to more modern catalogs such as the useful one by Hind, late Keeper of Prints at the British Museum. Mr. K. G. Boon of the Rijksmuseum has arranged a book of the complete etchings by date, and has challenged some earlier emendations. We have included the number of states, or versions made, of each etching, since this information may be valuable to the collector. Where there was a question of number of states available, we tended to rely on G. W. Nowell-Usticke's excellent recent book, *Rembrandt's Etchings: States and Values*. These and other helpful volumes may be found in the Bibliography.

Included are several etchings attributed to Rembrandt by Bartsch, but later challenged as to their authenticity by several eminent scholars. When modern critical opinion rejects the Rembrandt attribution, the etchings have been removed from the main body of work and placed in a special section, The Rejected Etchings.

Finally, one is face to face with Rembrandt, both artist and man. In art, it seems that first there is Rembrandt, and then there are all other artists. What is this quality that makes his name a synonym for genius to people who do not even recognize his works? We suggest that it is not a matter of technique, not a matter of subject, not a matter of style, but rather an all-pervasive humanity that illuminates even the meanest of these etchings. We have lived with these works for over a year as we prepared this book, and still we will find ourselves coming back to certain ones, noticing new details, opening our eyes to a play of light or shading. One etching may seize your imagination and then you will look at all the others in a new way . . . and then you will look at the things around you in a new way. Faces of children and beggars, hands of old women, heads of youths—all will be somehow different, more important, more real, more human, because of Rembrandt. The geography of the soul is explored and charted even in a tiny shepherd's face. Take the time to look carefully, and you will see the world through Rembrandt's eyes. It is a vision of truth, mercy, and humanity.

Rembrandt himself, in his later years, faced such a presentation as he pictured for Christ. The crowd of admirers and patrons melted away and the artist found himself presented to a void. In that void he kept working and kept faith with his own pursuit of truth. His celebrated bankruptcy had little effect on his production, although prints declined as he concentrated more and more on the luminous reality of his paintings. Death took Hendrickje, the support and inspiration of his old age, and Rembrandt worked on. Then his only surviving son, Titus, died. The darkness which the artist had created, fought, and shaped so often to his own purposes was taking more and more of the artist's life. The following year, 1669, the darkness was complete when Rembrandt died at sixty-three, stripped of the furnishings and the persons who had made his world, but left, to the end, with the inner light that gave that world its meaning.

After Rembrandt, the religious print—indeed, religious art in all forms—was no longer an enterprise for the serious artist. When, more than two centuries later, artists returned to Judaeo-Christianity for material, they returned to the personal, lonely encounter with religious truth, the mode of Rembrandt.

INTRODUCTION
BY FRANK GETLEIN

THE STORY OF REMBRANDT'S life and hard times is widely known; that's no reason not to tell it again. From one point of view, the poor man's life has been more influential than his art. There can't be a dozen artists in the world today really striving for the same total mastery of their art in either painting or prints; scarcely more share his faith in drawing. But what is conceived to be the moral lesson of Rembrandt's life is the faith of thousands.

The lesson is simple enough: Rembrandt died broke, unappreciated by his time because he was trying to do something new in art. Some years before his death his financial straits were so desperate he was forced into bankruptcy, he had his goods and chattels sold out from under him, and his entire artistic production was placed in the legal control of his mistress and his son. Within decades of his death the rehabilitation of Rembrandt began, and ever since, he has been thought one of the truly great. Moral: nothing succeeds like failure.

Remaining a failure, however, has become a difficult thing for an artist. Others have read the lesson of Rembrandt, too, among them many private purchasers of art and all museums and foundations. Today many a young artist concocts a solidly impenetrable manner only to find himself collected avidly, purchased by the Metropolitan, given a one-man show by The Museum of Modern Art, and packed off to Europe by the Guggenheim Foundation, there to meditate on the frustrations of being understood.

Both aspects of this interesting situation—the artist's determination to be unappreciated, and his public's determination to appreciate everything—derive ultimately from the ruin of Rembrandt, although both gained great strength from the somewhat later ruin of Rembrandt's countryman, Van Gogh. It is just possible, however, that this whole form-giving structure of contemporary art is based on a misreading of Rembrandt's ruin.

To begin with, bankruptcy is not entered into by the totally and permanently destitute. It results from an overextension of credit and expresses both the desire of the creditors to recover what they can from their debtor's existing capital, and the desire of the debtor to salvage what he can of the same capital. Credit, extended or overextended, implies a reasonable prospect of payment and hence the existence of a market for the goods or services of the debtor. For Rembrandt to get himself into bankruptcy at all, he had to be at least moderately successful in order to have credit to overextend, and successful for a long enough time to acquire the nonliquid capital that would make the bankruptcy worthwhile. Such was the case.

Rembrandt was widely and deeply appreciated during his life and from an early age. His financial failure came from his own deliberate withdrawal from a brilliant career as a fashionable portrait artist, and from his own spectacular mismanagement of his money. Insofar as the society of seventeenth-century Amsterdam bears any responsibility for the artist's ruin, that responsibility comes not from a failure to appreciate, but from a too facile appreciation. Rembrandt, from the time he was in his mid-twenties, enjoyed the full favor of fashion and the high pay that goes with the job. He happened to be a great artist and passed beyond fashion in his work at about the same time that fashion, inevitably, was turning elsewhere. He lived, however, as if he planned to be fashionable forever. He made imprudent investments, bought a luxurious house which became a huge burden, and poured his money into art collecting.

Beyond the obvious truth that estate management is a specialized trade, the lesson to be taken from Rembrandt's ruin is that, in anything more substantial than dressmaking or automobile manufacture, fashion is folly. Nothing can be done to discourage the operation of fashion in art, but the astonishing thing about the reparations-to-Rembrandt movement is that it places cultural institutions of immense dignity at the total service of fashion, for all the world as if they were General Motors.

Rembrandt's international fame, from his youth until a few decades ago, was based chiefly on his etchings. His approach to printmaking was radically different from that of his peers among painters, Raphael and Rubens. Raphael, through the engraver, Raimondi, and Rubens, through a well-organized workshop, both set up efficient businesses for the exploitation of their paintings. The print operation for both was rather like a road company of a Broadway hit. In Raimondi's shop and even more in Rubens' this led to a high degree of standardization of line, both for the purpose of translating paintings into prints and for ensuring the largest possible edition.

Both purposes were foreign to Rembrandt's print practice. Etching was for him an original art medium. He used it in conjunction with other techniques, such as drypoint and *retroussage*, that made for small editions. He also came to make succeeding states of his prints. A state of a print is created by changing the plate after the printing of some impressions. Proofs taken in the course of working on a plate are obviously a help to the artist, but in Rembrandt's work the existence of several states also reveals a genuine deepening of the original artistic vision. The change is sometimes quite radical, as in the different states reproduced of *Christ Presented to the People* and *The Three Crosses*.

With the almost solitary exception of Seghers, etching before Rembrandt's time was used as a fast way of making engravings. The artist drew his lines—or, more often, the craftsman drew them according to the artist's design—upon the acid-resistant ground laid over the copper, and the acid

4

simply did the work conventionally done by the engraver's strength and skill and cutting edge. The etched lines could be and were strengthened by subsequent engraving in the lines, as a pencil sketch may be traced over in ink. The result of such etching was to destroy the peculiar character engraving derives from the resistance of copper to the cutting edge, and, at the same time, to leave unexplored the new technical and expressive possibilities of etching.

That exploration, Rembrandt made his own. The two outstanding new possibilities of etching that Rembrandt made into infinitely delicate instruments of expression were the increased directness of working on the plate, and the greatly extended range of light and dark. The first comes from the ease with which the etcher's needle moves through its ground; the second, from the gradations possible by controlling the time various portions of the exposed copper are subject to the corrosive acid. Drypoint and its rich burr add to both effects.

Rembrandt was not the last religious artist, but he was in the last generation in which it was possible for great artists to find in Christianity thematic material for their complete engagement intellectually and complete fulfillment artistically. Among his contemporaries were Rubens (rather older) in Flanders, and Zurbarán and Velázquez in Spain. In the Catholic countries, the strong impulse of the Counter Reformation gave a renewed and prolonged life to religious art, but that life expired as the impulse hardened into the fanaticism of the religious war. In Protestant Holland, the situation of religious art was more complicated. There was a basic Puritanical suspicion of church art; this, combined with a rising class of entrepreneurial bourgeois, created conditions favorable to portrait, still-life, and landscape painting. On the other hand, aided by Holland's successful war of independence against Spain and by the great growth of Netherlands wealth, there was a widespread feeling that the Dutch were really the chosen people of God; this led to some interest in paintings and prints of Old Testament scenes, wherein the proto-Dutch of Palestine defied their enemies and carried out their mission. Like other aspects of Puritanism, this belief in one's own election by God turned up shortly in New England, but was not accompanied by much in the line of art.

Against that background of changing religious patterns in Europe, with the new pattern leading to the complete separation of church and art, Rembrandt created a new artistic embodiment of Europe's Christian faith. His new religious art was intensely personal in all the ways that word is used of an artist. His etchings of the traditional Gospel subjects present a view of the sacred persons and events with which the personality of the viewer, led by the personality of the artist, is brought into intimate contact. The relative informality of the etched line may be cited as making this possible: it expresses so clearly the movement of the artist's hand holding the needle. Rembrandt's own religious faith can as readily be cited as impelling his mastery of the delicate means of etching.

For that faith, as seen in the etchings, is quite different from the faith expressed in the religious art of his contemporaries and predecessors. Rembrandt's is based upon a deep understanding of and sympathy for the person of Jesus. There is, in complete humility, something of an identification between the artist and the Jesus of the prints. This is a radical change from the public religious art of the Italians, the Spanish, and the Flemish. The basic religious relationship is not that of the Catholics, between the individual and the Church, nor that of the Protestants, between the individual and the community of the Elect. Rather, it is between the individual and Jesus as presented in the Gospel. The greatest of Rembrandt's religious etchings are not representations of events, but profound commentaries on them, expressing the personal religious experience of a sensitive, devout mind.

The sensitive line reflecting that mind appears from the first in the little self-portraits that Rembrandt etched. Variations of clothing are tried, variations of expression. Constant is the inquiring gaze of the soul into itself. The early etchings of the artist's mother combine complete realism with deep affection.

Two religious prints, made in Rembrandt's early years of prosperity, contrast the two general methods he was exploring to make etching yield its expressive possibilities. *The Return of the Prodigal Son* is all line, although the lines here and there come close together. The scratching of the needle picks out the gaunt, angular, and exhausted form of the youth, the heartbroken compassion of the father. The whole house—architecturally as well as in the persons of the family—comes down to meet the boy. The postures and gestures distinguish clearly and subtly among the degrees of welcome. The basic movement down, meeting the boy's desperate imploring, is softly strengthened by the planes of the house—solidly established in so few lines—meeting with the ascent of the steps. The very angle of the wanderer's staff plays its part in the expressive structure of the total group. Through the archway, the faintest of lines—drawn as if upon the air—suggest the dust of the road and the heat of the journey home. The parable of the prodigal son, related in the New Testament as an analogy of the kingdom of heaven, has been made an intensely human drama of repentance and forgiveness.

In *The Angel Appearing to the Shepherds,* the whole emotional and intellectual burden of the print is carried, not by line, but by the sharp contrast between light and dark, and by the subtle shifting through the degrees of one or the other. There are two great centers of light, the angels on high and the shepherds below, who are hearing the news of Christ's birth. Between the two flows a deep gulf of dark, almost like an impassable river from the upper right to the lower left of the print. The point of the incident, in Rembrandt's view as in that of most Christians, is that the gulf between man and God, impassable for theological and historical reasons, has been bridged by the appearance of the angels over Bethlehem and the tidings they brought to mankind.

Within that dark gulf may be dimly seen a landscape of the earth, with light faintly glowing along hills, trees, a town, and a river spanned by a bridge. As those forms exist within the darkness, so the angelic forms exist within the light. The two poles of light in the print are by no means equal.

It is quite clear that the light on the shepherds, although it frightens them and their flocks, is a faint projection from the heavenly light of the angels. Shepherds and beasts are made visible in part by the shadows upon them. The angels are light, becoming more clearly differentiated as they move toward the earth, less as they move toward the light. The faint lines in the very center of the light suggest swarms of cherubim emerging from absolute light as the town and the river emerge from pitch dark.

The angels tumbling out of light reach a climax of visibility and are fixed in the figure of the foremost angel, standing on a cloud and addressing the shepherds. The shepherds, scattering from the unexpected light, are climaxed in the shepherd, who, though frightened, does not run. The bodies of the animals express varieties of confusion: some bolt, some are fixed in their tracks. This is intensified in the reactions of the other men. One runs blindly away. One falls on his back, overcome. Two look on, transfixed. The central shepherd is their focal point. He and the announcing angel are two poles between which leaps the spark of God's news for man.

Landscape, all but lost in *The Angel Appearing*, is the whole subject in two of Rembrandt's finest etchings. In an age when, as ever since, a landscape was relatively sure-fire, Rembrandt etched very few of them. Out of a total production of about three hundred prints, there are fewer than thirty landscapes. In most of them he went beyond the faithful reproduction of scene.

The Three Trees is based on the same dramatic play of light against dark and dark against light as *The Angel Appearing*. The trees are a dark mass against the sky. The light of the sky is cut in on along the top, to some extent in the upper right and most strongly in the sharp slanting lines on the left, in order to shape the light to fit the dark at its center. Yet neither light sky nor dark trees are stark. From the almost total darkness of the small triangular area in the upper left corner, the sky gets progressively lighter as it gets nearer the trees, yet it is never free of lines. The trees, so dark against the white sky, are nevertheless full of the play of light and shadow within their silhouettes. This is true also of the dark bank on which the trees stand. The light of the sky is continued in the bit of reflection in the foreground stream, and then is used as land light as the artist, with few lines and an amazing sense of graduated distance, takes us across the whole flat land of Holland.

The flatness and stretch of the land beneath the infinity of sky are even more magnificently shown in *The Goldweigher's Field*. The light and dark contrast is very subtle, much of it coming from the expert use of drypoint. The lines, delicate but strong, pick out a host of details which, when you look at them, become houses, ditches, peasants at work, and, when you don't, are simply part of the terrain sweep of Holland.

Faust in His Study deploys the light and dark of the etched plate around a central activity of Rembrandt's life, the pursuit of truth through the practice of an art. The legend of Faust, as swaggered by Marlowe and intoned by Goethe, is far from the tense quiet of the scholar's room. This Faust is not after his lost youth, nor does he seek a peep show of history. He wants the secret behind life, and we see him at a moment of illumination. He rises from his chair, his hand still holding what could be the instrument of either scholar or printmaker. The magical disk glows against the light of all outdoors and makes the sunlight through the window seem dim. Even paler is the light on the celestial globe in the lower right. The living light, given its quality from the repeated but irregular lines with which it is broken, glows in two places: the disk and its radiance, and the face and form of Faust. The intensity of light is raised by the richly textured darkness. Quartered at the center of the disk are four letters from an occasion in which Rembrandt himself, in the pursuit of his art, was to find a measure of truth. They are the INRI that Pilate placed above the head of the dying Christ.

Rembrandt's small etchings of the childhood of Jesus are done without the dramatic contrast of light and dark that so dazzles in *The Angel Appearing to the Shepherds.* Yet within that narrower range there is all the contrast needed to carry Rembrandt's thought and feeling about the childhood of Jesus.

In *The Flight into Egypt,* the relatively heavy, coarse lines depict the little family fleeing from the hatred of Herod, the Palestinian puppet king determined to kill the child prophesied as "king." The thick lines do indeed convey the visual and tactile qualities of homespun cloth on Joseph, the foliage overhead, the rough coat of the donkey. Spaced farther apart, the lines are used for shadow on the mantle and cloak of Mary; spaced nearer together, they coalesce into the dark forest behind the travelers. Yet the roughness of the lines has in it also something of the roughness of the journey: the abrupt departure, the weary road, the uncomfortable conditions, the fatigue, and the danger behind. This is not to suggest the use of a deliberate symbolic language of line, only that the mind and heart have equal share with the eye and hand in controlling the point upon the copper.

Certainly the line is quite different in the *Christ Seated, Disputing with the Doctors.* Massed lines are used mainly for shadow. The figures, especially those of Christ and the principal "doctors," are chiefly conveyed by outline, and all lines are more delicate. There is variety of response in the faces of those listening, but the responses suggested are all within a limited range. The focus is on the face and form of the boy Jesus. His sweet-gravity is summed up in a few lines, and the unique moment is characterized by the earnest gesture of the hand and the boyish swing of the right leg. The event is the single emergence of Jesus from the so-called "hidden life" led at Nazareth. The family had gone up to Jerusalem for Passover. Joseph and Mary missed Jesus on the return trip with a group of pilgrims. They returned to the capital and found him, according to St. Luke, "in the temple, sitting in the midst of the doctors, hearing them and asking them questions."

Christ Between His Parents, Returning from the Temple follows that incident. The tone of the lines to some extent combines that of the other two. The background, darkening foliage in the first, the flat wall of the temple in the second, open now to the hilly Judean landscape. There is a left-to-right progression within the background from near to far and from dark to light. As in *The Goldweigher's Field,* the terrain reveals, on examination, houses, a village, a pool of water, men and animals, all blended into the landscape on first glance. Returning to Nazareth, Jesus explained, "I must be about my Father's business," but nevertheless he accompanied Mary and Joseph to the small town where he lived for more than a decade and a half before he began the public ministry. The curve of the background suggests abstractly something of that situation, but it exists at its most powerful in the aspiration of the boy's face between the submission of Mary and the patient humility of Joseph.

In dealing with the preaching ministry of Christ, Rembrandt created what is beyond doubt the most famous etching and quite likely the most famous and best loved print in existence. *Christ Healing the Sick* (the "Hundred Guilder Print") combines several incidents in the Gospels. The lame and the blind are led, carried, and wheeled. The poor have the Gospel preached to them and the children are welcomed. In the shadow of the city wall of Jerusalem Christ preaches; the light goes forth into the darkness, and the whole composition moves from both sides to the preacher. Nearest him are the poor and oppressed, who approach him in hope and trust. On the left, as in the print of the boy in the temple, the faces register the degrees of skeptical response. On the right, apparently in the gate known as the "Needle's Eye," a camel has difficulty getting through; the beast's master wears the turban of a "rich man," who, according to Christ, has similar difficulty entering the kingdom of heaven. The face of Jesus shines with patience and love in the midst of the people he has come to save and the forces that will destroy him.

The destruction is accomplished in *The Three Crosses*. The print exists in numerous states. The changes are the most drastic ever introduced in a print scene that remains essentially the same from state to state. The light changes radically. Characters vanish, others appear. Christ on the cross remains constant, but to look from the early state to the later is to watch the body grow emaciated and approach death. The overall light darkens, as a result of which the light behind Christ's head and down his body takes on a different quality, as if it came from within.

It has been suggested that in executing and printing the succeeding states, Rembrandt intended a series on the Crucifixion. It may have been. The prints themselves speak powerfully of an ever more deeply realized conviction, taking its progress in the act of working on the plate.

The other celebrated example of Rembrandt's changing his basic image as the plate passed from state to state is the *Christ Presented to the People*. The moment is Pilate's presentation of the beaten-up victim to the crowd in the hope that the visible evidence of punishment will placate those who demanded the death sentence. The changes from the early state to the later are all directed toward the same end. There are some architectural changes, the combined effect of which is to move the whole tableau slightly forward, nearer the viewer. Lines have been added everywhere and earlier lines have been further etched, so that both darkness and solidity have come upon the buildings. In the early state, the whole building half-resembles a stage set; in the later, it bears down with the weight of masonry upon the victim presented and upon the spectator. The victim himself has grown more pitiable, more abject. Pilate, from the sympathetic evasion of the early state, has passed into grossness.

The most remarkable change, however, is in the lower third of the plate. Not only the crowd but the very ground it stood on has been taken away. Instead, a black gulf, punctuated by the arches of the platform, yawns before the artist and the viewer alike. We are no longer watching a simple historical event, Rembrandt makes clear. We are taking part in one. Christ, beaten and passive, is presented not to a Judean crowd of the first century, but to a Dutch individual of the seventeenth, and to those who have come since then to the print.

A RAMBLING STORY

Van Dongen
here
recounts
the life of
REMBRANDT
and writes,
in this connection,
about Holland,
women,
and art.

A RAMBLING STORY

AROUND 1600, HOLLAND IS A REPUBLIC. The Dutch are rugged and strong men who are always fighting against the weather and especially against the sea, that wench who requires rogues as lovers.

The country is flat and wide, green and blue; its boundaries stretch farther, when one thinks he's reached them; neither Holland nor the Dutch know the frontiers.

Moreover, the natives of this foreign country always travel around the world. Their strength is amazing; their daring wholehearted. On the sea lanes, they sometimes meet other mariners, other rogues, and then they fight, since they want to be free and to go wherever they see fit. Freedom is their ideal; the battle their justification.

A legend tells that the rogues of Holland have a famous ship, feared by all navigators—a phantom ship, *The Flying Dutchman*—which never has been boarded by any enemy, and that this boat still sails the seas.

Amsterdam is their den. There, they amass all the booty stolen from others.

In 1638, Pierre-Henri, captain of a flotilla of rogues, takes and returns with a whole Spanish treasure fleet, filled with booty that the Spanish had obviously stolen.

Captain Ter Heyde fights the English fleet in 1653 near Dunes, and crosses the Strait of Dover with a broom hung from his mainmast to show that they swept them up.

Thus, and always, it is the theft at sword-point that is most important, and the Dutch are proud of their armed deeds; they honor and glorify their heroes.

Nothing ever changes in this world, if methods do not. It is strength and cunning that rule and create.

The people live as if in an aquarium. Everything is an artifice and a work of art. The land is below sea level; the sky is wider than the sea and land combined. Fog and clouds permeate the houses and the minds of the inhabitants. Many men are seized by fevers, and there is a bit of madness in everyone. Nervous disorders are widespread; rheumatism is hereditary, as is an extreme sensibility and sentimentality.

In these foreign countries where sexual pleasures are experienced only in well-hidden places, where beds are hidden first behind curtains and then heavy wooden doors, where the inhabitants are farmers, morality is strict and puritanical; nature is stronger than reason and often twists morality.

In the countryside along the Rhine, near Leiden, in a low, small house that seems to float in the air, lives a miller with his family. He leads a rural life, and satisfies his simple desires by cultivating his garden. He waters it well; therefore he is rewarded for his care by the birth of several children.

The last born is a boy, who is named Rembrandt.

Several years pass, and this lad is half a child of the nation and half peasant. His parents, like all other parents, dream for him a condition better than their own. His mother, more than his father, wants him to become "someone"—a scholar, a judge, or a burgomaster.

His father doesn't know what he wants, nor does the boy know, and he cares little about the future; he likes to play, to fight, and to run in the fields with his friends. But he is often alone, and he roams around his father's mill.

Very happily, he escapes and goes to Leiden, a city where there are, for him, all types of unknown pleasures: there are crowds, there is a lot of noise, there are mountebanks, people who trade everything, shops where one can see amassed treasures. Nobody notices his presence there, and he can roam as he likes and let himself go with the currents of the crowd. He has a good time there, and he dreams. He dreams, but, with his sensible mind, he dreams especially of making money. In the shops he sees many beautiful things; he spends hours in front of pictures. He is attracted by marvelous objects: paintings that are more beautiful than anything else, that are tangible dreams of happiness and of beauty within his grasp, and that he would like to possess.

If it were only possible to steal these paintings for which he lusts! But it is difficult, for one must be large and strong to be a thief, and he is small and is afraid of his father, who has such big hands, who is so strong, and who carries large sacks of wheat with ease. He dares not encourage his father's wrath, for a slap from his father would perhaps kill him, and once dead, he couldn't see any paintings or anything any more. There is also his mother, but he isn't afraid of her; she seems to him to be very weak next to his father, who is a formidable and inviolable person.

He will therefore never be able to carry off the paintings and all that they represent: nudes, palaces, dogs, landscapes, flowers, fruits, objects of all types, and thus all the beautiful things in the world. He would like all that for himself, in a hiding place where neither his parents nor anyone else would search.

There is only one small room in his parents' attic. He goes there very excitedly and with his head full of dreams. In a trunk he has a small piece of painted crockery, chipped but beautiful; an image raised from the pages of a book; some feathers, belonging to a rooster, which he found in the hen-house; some pebbles that, when wet with the tongue, seem to contain gold; and a glass ball that is a miraculous object.

But all the things that he found so beautiful before seem rather small and worthless since he saw Leiden; his room is so bare with its whitewashed walls; everything around him seems so poor. His treasure is no longer a treasure. He thinks only of the paintings that he admired in the shops in the city, of the botanical garden with its exotic flowers, of the armor, of the rugs, of the cloth embroidered with gold, and of the jewels. His room is nothing, his parents' house is small; even his father doesn't seem as important.

He spends entire days dreaming, and his mother begins to worry, she who would like to make something of this boy whom she cherishes. She scrimps in order to send him to the Leiden Gymnasium, where he will study with other young men, where he will be in with fashionable society. What an honor for his family! The miller's son will be a gentlemen with good manners, and be learned—very learned. His mother will be proud of him. She speaks of him often to his father, who would prefer to keep him in his mill, to make him a miller with large calloused hands and strong muscles. Gentlemen don't know how to do anything, and why learn how to read *all* books? The miller can scarcely read, and reads poorly; he reads as he prays and he reads only the Bible. That is a sacred book; the others are useless. Moreover, reading is good for only five minutes; after that, one should light a pipe and take a walk in the fields or go to the tavern to find other men and to chat, to make a little noise, and to feel alive. He doesn't dream; he acts: he grinds his wheat, sells it, and supports his small family.

His mother obtains permission to go with her son to Leiden in order to accompany him while he registers at the Gymnasium. She is very glad, as she has so much confidence in the teachers' knowledge that she believes her dream is already realized once her son attends this school.

Rembrandt is also very happy: for him, it is an opportunity to spend every day in Leiden, to contemplate the paintings every day, to try to do some, to observe the people in the city, and to have his own room. And, above all, he can paint. He knows he will never be a scholar or a burgomaster; he guesses that his parents will not see their dreams come true. He is still an affectionate young man, and sometimes he is bothered by the trouble he gives his parents by not listening to them, by not yielding to their small desires, to their miniscule dreams that have been stunted by their sedentary and honest life. He does not like his studies: he sketches on his notebooks, he paints in his room, and he makes very little progress in school. His logic does not comprehend the beauty of learning to read Latin when everyone around him speaks Dutch. The teachers punish him; he's a mischievous student, but in this country, where one never gives up hope, they don't hold a grudge against a naughty student. If he prefers to sketch rather than to learn his lessons, that is his business; each person must determine his own life.

His mother is not happy: she sees her hopes vanish; she speaks about this to her husband, who, to avoid discussion, says that everything will work out all right. But it doesn't. Rembrandt becomes more bizarre. He plays truant from school, or shuts himself in his room, where he paints, even at night by candlelight.

Painting is the only thing he does well, because it is the only thing he does with passion, and already he has a small reputation among his friends.

His parents, despondent over the slowness of his studies and regretting the money already spent, take him out of school; but Rembrandt no longer wants to return to the mill. He stays in his room in Leiden, and tries to earn a living by selling his paintings.

He paints, he dreams, and his whims are stretched to their extremes. He wishes with a superhuman force. He desires all possible powers and riches. He already knows that his dream is not for possessing the world, but he wants to realize this dream: to create beauty, to flood the earth with it, and to give everything; to render all people happy with pictures—paintings that can transform a modest hovel into a stately palace. He wants to make all mankind happy as he himself is happy on seeing a beautiful thing.

Yet he is afraid of life and of men; he would like to stay home, to live quietly under the sail of the mill, in the calm of the countryside, to become a miller, to live like his father; or to realize his mother's dream of becoming a clothier, a scholar or a burgomaster. But something within him revolts against this weakness. Again he brightens up, and a new dream comes to him. A large winged white horse, rearing against the wind, flies over him. It's like the guardian angel of the Bible, it's like his genie. He sees it, and believes in it. He sees and believes now that in him is germinating that which is the most beautiful in life; that in him is incarnated the great will of a people who fought for centuries against the elements, against itself, against others, and he feels its power. He believes that he is the spirit of his nation, a type of monster; and he knows that there is no glory in being this spirit. He knows that it's like a game but he has no choice. Fate sent him the role! Red, odd—bet and lose.

Jacques de Swanenburch is an established painter in Leiden. He is a very talented man who has studied in Italy and married a Neapolitan girl. It is the vogue to go to Italy, and the Dutch painters who studied there are impregnated with Italian art. Their paintings are very fashionable. Swanenburch's paintings sell well, and he takes on students who grind his colors, prepare his frames and his canvases, and learn from their master the art of painting.

Rembrandt, who is already a skillful painter, finds it easy to be taken on by Swanenburch, and he earns a living. He works there with other young men, among whom is Jean Liévens. There is naturally a camaraderie established among the students, and Liévens often visits Rembrandt while he is working in his own room after his day's work with his teacher. Rembrandt does not admire Swanenburch greatly, and he is already separated from him by his way of interpreting different subjects. He has a great skill, and soon he feels sufficiently capable to go out on his own. He is not made to work for others; he is touchy and doesn't accept observations and corrections.

Rembrandt is standing in front of an easel in his room, which also serves as his studio. The white-washed walls are covered with sketches and notations, and on one of the walls is an optical illusion of a long staircase that winds and climbs up to the black-beamed ceiling. Colored rags and cloths are scattered about, and the window is partly inaccessible because of piles of cloth and papers. The room is his laboratory. There he captures and directs, according to his inclinations, the light from outside.

A luminous ray crosses the room like a sword through a body. The rest is in shade, lit only by the obscure light of reflections.

In the bright ray of light is a table on which are set up several objects: a skull sitting on a Bible, next to it a globe, and a glass of water with tulips in it.

Rembrandt is painting a *vanitas*.

In a corner near the window, on another table, sit engraver's tools with a large open box filled with sketches and prints. Liévens looks at them.

On the floor, turned against the wall, are canvases. Hanging on a folding screen on the other side of the window are half-finished paintings: a study, *Lot and his Daughters*; another study, *The Eunuch's Baptism*.

In an obscure corner, on a bed, is seated an old beggar who is sanctimoniously smoking a short pipe.

Some chairs, some small benches on which there are several books (Huygens' poetry), more cloth, a large overcoat of red velvet with a fur collar, and an unrecognizable curio form the décor of the room.

That which dominates all is the build of the young painter, standing, his back in full light and his face in the shadow.

If an American boxer let his hair grow, and wore a moustache and a goatee, he would look like Rembrandt. A heavyweight boxer is the best person physically to play the role of Rembrandt in the movies, because Rembrandt has an artist's head on an athlete's body.

It is generally men like this who like to squabble, to drink, to sing sentimental songs, and to dress ridiculously in a woman's plumed and feathered hat. They are photogenic, and the slightest emotion is inscribed instantaneously on their variable faces. A simple toothache bothers them greatly; all the sadness and suffering of mankind, which likes to drink and pick up women's skirts, are inscribed on their physiognomy.

Jean Liévens, who works with Rembrandt, using the same models, contents himself for the moment by looking at his friend's sketches because the ribald girl who is to pose for one of Lot's daughters did not come, preferring to roam about the town. The old beggar who is posing as the blessed man Lot waits without asking for more money, but Rembrandt works on his *vanitas* with feverishness because he wants an etching by Lucas that he saw in a secondhand store.

He is never satisfied with what he does; he doesn't know when a painting is done; for him nothing is ever completely finished. This painting does not please him; but he wants the etching, and on the advice of Liévens, he signs it and dates it 1626. He hangs his work on a nail to let it dry, and picks up another painting he has begun, *Judas Returning the Price of Betrayal.*

But the man who is posing for Judas left to go to bed with the girl posing for Lot's daughter. The old beggar can't take the place of Judas. Rembrandt is furious. He pushes the poor old man, who is not responsible for the affairs of the other models. He takes his coat and hat and leaves, slamming the door behind him, without caring about his friend Liévens, who is beginning to get used to these whims.

Rembrandt has an unbearable personality: the slightest annoyance makes him furious; he is authoritarian and weak at the same time. He never accepts his models' not being there on time; yet, at the same time, he does not want to encroach upon their freedom; he understands that they prefer to tipple rather than to pose soberly as models for biblical characters. He understands the confusion and effervescence of others.

He himself is not orderly, and he too is full of effervescence. His head is filled with thoughts, his body is full of desires, his heart overflows with fondness. He believes that he likes no one and that no one likes him.

His tenderness goes toward animals. He knows an old work horse: a large, good, old white animal with a head that hangs sadly toward the ground and, in that head, two large quiet eyes ringed with the black of suffering, and on his nose a blob of delicate pink. To be this old horse, to be led around by a peasant, to look humbly at the ground while letting the rain fall drop by drop on his large white back, to suffer in silence, to fall down under a yoke, to be an animal, led to the slaughterhouse without a will—that is life.

But life is also a revolt against life: a strong, warm gust of wind; the flame coming from the nostrils of a proud and touchy animal who paws the ground, who runs off, tramples everything under foot, jumps obstacles—a large winged stallion who caracoles in the air, a demon horse who climbs over the clouds and flies toward the light in order to join with the sun and create a deity. . . . He will be these two animals: he feels within himself this duality, these two principles; and he knows that he will be forever tossed about between the submissiveness of the meek and the toughness of the powerful.

He goes into a house of prostitution, and in a back room, on a dirty straw bed, he gratifies his anguish. He feels undulating beneath him warm and fiery life.

Now Rembrandt wants to learn, wants to know. The mischievous boy from the Leiden Gymnasium now reads everything on which he sets his eyes, but especially the Bible, which remains for him the most entertaining book there is, the book that reveals all, that explains his dreams, that transports him into eternity and into a dreamworld full of the most glorious imagery: the most complete and the best portrayer of life.

He reads and draws. He paints, and he forgets the life that is not as beautiful as his dreams, for he converts his dreams into imagery, into paintings. He brings into his room paupers, sick people, lepers; a prostitute poses as the Virgin Mary for him; an old beggar poses as a famous priest; other beggars pose as Saint Joseph, Simon, and all of heaven; and thus he paints in his small room *Presentation in the Temple* with a dreamlike background, inspired by the Bible, or a *Holy Family*, with the same models. His art and his idealism ennoble his models; their realism keeps them from too much bombast; his country's light, his love of life, his tormented youth, his troubled spirit, his impatience and ardor to realize his dreams, inspire his masterpieces. His ardent youth retreats from nothing, and inside his biblical compositions, he draws and engraves images that are very realistic, as crude and as direct as the language of his models whom he gathers from anywhere. His fame grows rapidly, and amateur painters, who are numerous in Holland, come to him, buy his works, order his paintings.

Even from Amsterdam people come to him. He often takes his own paintings there, and then strolls around: sees some paintings, buys some knickknacks, some cloth and some foreign things; for in Amsterdam, more so than in Leiden, things are livelier and there are beautiful girls who are well provided for by the privateers and the traveling merchants. A beautiful girl who is well dressed and who is sweet smelling is more receptive to taking off her clothes than is a slut in rags.

There is, in Amsterdam, a quarter near the port where the mariners live and the prostitutes room, where life is fast and loose; here Rembrandt likes to spend the money he earns from his paintings, but he does not go there only to soothe his fever; he sees life. This lonely person likes life so much that he throws himself into it headlong, and he flounders in it until satiety.

Afterward, he returns pale and penniless to Leiden, to his studio, to his paintings, to his dreams and his visions. His body calmed for several days, he dreams of another life—more beautiful, perhaps more harmonious, but harder to attain. He dreams of a wife, a beautiful woman; of family life, beautiful children; of a dispassionate sexual life; of a well-kept house—of all the things that are opposed to his versatile personality, his vagabond spirit, and his ardent heart. And his dreams always caracole above him.

Only in his painting does he remain clairvoyant. In them he can let himself go; too bad if one does not understand him or if one condemns him; and if one thinks he's crazy, so much the better. In his painting he can show all his love, and he has violent passions like a young animal. He is so full of health, so brutal and so tender at the same time, so ardent and so daring, that for his placid and logical contemporaries he is a sort of monster. And he is an artist, a calm creator of images. One understands the disorder, the vigor, and the bestiality of the great ones: the captains, the merchants, the warriors; the people who return home with gold and other good things to accumulate or eat; but for a dreamer, a poet, this seems monstrous and immoral. With his young fame in painting, with his glory, rises at the same time a legend of disorder and unbalance.

However, no young man ever worked more than he, no one was attracted as much as he to his work, no one cared about others more than he. All he does, he does in order to paint better. If he reads, if he studies, if he is interested in everything, if he goes anywhere, everywhere and always he goes there as a pioneer, searching for something that may help him to better understand life so that he can better realize his dreams.

He has several orders for portraits in Amsterdam, and between sittings he noses about the second-hand shops, looking for objects to satisfy his collector's taste. But always with the thought of using in his paintings the objects he finds, and likes, and buys; and when he acquires others' works, it is to discover in them their secrets and to enjoy their beauty. To create beauty, to be surrounded by beautiful things and to live among them: for him, this is the height of pleasure. But more and more he needs ornamental paintings to embellish and to frame his young and ardent love for life.

He earns money, but money is not a beautiful thing, and then he has nothing more pressing to do than to spend it.

During his stays in Amsterdam — he stays with a merchant who buys several paintings from him — he has no desire for money. He finds it easy to alleviate his excess dreams in the city. He lives like a sailor on a spree. He lets himself go indiscreetly, and he would be almost happy if he didn't always feel within him that fire, that fever burning him, that pity that he has for the poor and the unfortunate, that compassion for the so-called rich and powerful, that arrogance which makes him prefer solitude to being with someone, that self-confidence which renders him unbearable to others.

If he were not always preoccupied, so absorbed in his visions—if he did not have that fury of painting that prevented him from enjoying, like others, the pleasures of the transitory world, he would perhaps be happy; but in reality he is very unhappy. Nothing satisfies him: neither his paintings nor his short-lived love affairs. He dreams of a more perfect and more beautiful love, but he has not yet found the object of this dream. There is the Muse, the painting, which takes the best from him; to the women, to his wife, he will give what is left, and he feels strong enough to satisfy both.

Amsterdam in the seventeenth century is like Venice was formerly and like Paris is today: a city of the *nouveaux riches.* It is natural for a man to show and want to affirm his power. The artists in Amsterdam receive many orders for portraits, because all the merchants, the bourgeoisie, satisfied and happy with themselves, are proud of being able to say, on showing their portraits, "That's me."

Rembrandt receives more and more orders, and he decides to settle in Amsterdam. There he paints portraits of the bourgeoisie, but his paintings do more than just represent his models, and, through painting the bourgeoisie, he does a sort of communist painting. Free thought and expression are permitted in this great city.

What happiness Rembrandt finds in being able to travel the entire world just by walking on Amsterdam's docks! From the whole world flow to Amsterdam the wealth, the seekers of fortune, the seekers of truth, and the seekers of beauty. Art can flourish only in a rich land, and Amsterdam is the world's storehouse of affluence. Ostentatious merchants rule there as masters. Naturally, these people turn to Rubens or to Van Dyck, whom they understand better, rather than to Rembrandt, who is too revolutionary for most of the connoisseurs; but wealth is so great that there is room for everyone.

There are in Amsterdam, like everywhere else, people who look for the bizarre, the unknown, the new, or that which seems so to them. There are even very distinguished people who are really connoisseurs, and who like things for their beauty alone. Therefore, Rembrandt, during his debut in Amsterdam, is still not yet the separated man, the solitary hero whom one can follow. He is only a very good painter, especially in his portraits; he is not yet the monster he will later be. His way of life is already very censured and already is doing him harm. However, the orders for his portraits flow in, and he has little time to spend with wretches and with the poems in the Bible.

As soon as he has a moment, he goes on a spree; he goes to the sailors' dens, he draws beggars; and to him those who possess nothing, not even prejudices, are the richest people.

And this Rembrandt, in spite of his success, in spite of the money he earns, often wanders, with a troubled spirit and a head full of dreams, in the streets of bad repute and in the deserted countryside, where he feels, when he has emptiness in his soul, less alone than among the rich merchants. A great uneasiness is in him; often a deep neurasthenia tortures him; and while walking alone, across the countryside, or roaming around the warm streets, he finds peace, and he can think about his painting.

One thinks him to be happy: he is already famous, his paintings are sold. But painting is deceiving his soul, painting is a dream, and real life is the realization of one's dreams. He wants to live, to enjoy life, to inhale it completely, to partake fully of its fruits, to fornicate with women, to sing, to shout, to drink. He dreams of living in a palace full of riches, of reading the Bible while caressing a beautiful woman, of going to sleep drunk with wine and love and with his head resting on a woman's stomach. But he has no woman, only women: prostitutes of good will, mistresses for a moment and diversions. He remains unsatisfied after the best debaucheries, unhappy with himself, with his hard-to-please body, and with his distressed soul. He stumbles and bumps himself, everywhere and always, against the prejudices, the laws, the frontiers, and the narrowness of everything surrounding him.

The country in which he lives is a northern country, and its inhabitants—those merchants, scoundrels, correct people, parasites of the sea, slave-traders, captains, scholars, thinkers, mystics, Jews—come from everywhere. He is their poet, their spirit. He lives for them, suffers for them, but they are unaware of him, because to them, what is an artist, a dreamer, a poet? For them, life is possessing everything: they neither have the time nor the desire to think; they live and search for the means to augment their power.

Rembrandt returns to his purchaser, Monsieur de Châtelhiboux, and finds a blonde and blooming girl living there. Le Hibou introduces his cousin Saskia to him. For an honest reason he has brought her from the provinces. Saskia is the daughter of a rich Frisian lawyer; she is personable, intelligent, and dressed with good taste.

They desire each other. Soon, the reciprocal attraction becomes stronger than propriety. Neither religion nor puritanical customs could have prevented them. One night, Rembrandt, instead of going to his own room, enters Saskia's room, where she has been waiting for him for many nights with a palpitating heart.

Even the oriental storytellers find themselves impotent when trying to describe the beatitudes of two young lovers. The following night, the game begins again; and following the embraces, through the entire night, the lovers warble sweet words, swear eternal love, and make plans. During the day, Rembrandt paints; he is a subdued man now, he abandons the taverns. He does portraits of Saskia. He is happy day and night.

Saskia is also happy but worried at the same time: she is afraid of her family, afraid of the sins she is committing so spiritedly, and especially afraid of becoming pregnant and disgracing her family. In her closed sleeping alcove, in the dark and out of fear, she dares to speak of marriage with her lover. Rembrandt is a gallant man. He accepts the idea of marriage; in order to please his mistress he will do anything foolish. That very day he asks for her hand.

The problems begin right away, because Saskia's parents are rich and, as marriage is always a business transaction for the rich, they begin to talk with concern. Rembrandt wants to marry in order to please his lover, but he does not have to also marry her parents or Le Hibou. He sees that, in obtaining Saskia, he will have to submit to her family, he will have to become a bourgeois like them, manage wealth, talk with businessmen, submit to all the boring and ridiculous customs inherent in a bourgeois marriage, listen to a minister's sermon, make calls, occupy himself with formalities, sign papers—all that to be able to go to bed legally with his wife. There is nothing beautiful, no poetry, in that. He has a fear, he is pessimistic about this commercial marriage, but he loves his mistress. He is in love. He has an irresistible desire to have this woman for himself as completely as possible: to have a beautiful model, a woman to adorn in rare clothes and jewels, a woman to strip, to love to satiety. He is a coward, and he lets himself be married. The ceremony is boring, like all official ceremonies; but after the wedding, he can love his mistress with the permission of the minister and her relatives.

The next day he causes a scandal because he wants to paint Saskia nude.

Saskia, in spite of her love and perhaps because of it, notices that reality does not correspond with the dreams of a well-bred girl. The clandestine nights when her lover came stealthily to find her, when her heart beat with anxiety, with fear and desire, were beautiful; and it was pleasant to curl up in the arms of her lover, to give herself and to receive; because it was not an artist, it was not Rembrandt whom she welcomed, but forbidden, divine, and invisible love. It was something beyond her and against which she was helpless; it was the ephemeral blooming of life's flower. Marriage reaped the flower, and Saskia thought that it was good that way.

Love has flourished for an instant in the body of this woman, but man's religion, laws, and reason soon trample the flowers and leave her only with weakness. Her husband, having become her property by a legal act, is now only her husband. Her love became unseemly by the blessing of a minister and the participation of the civil authorities: security has ruined her. Rembrandt has not changed; he remains his wife's lover. The minister's sermons, the papers of the notary and the state—this registry office for couples about to be married—has not the slightest influence on his love.

Rembrandt paints; Rembrandt dreams. He loves his wife, and decks her out in beautiful clothes, gives her all she desires, and thinks she is happy. He is too wrapped up in his painting and in his love to admit that his wife could desire anything else: he does not even think about it. He is happy; he paints and he sings.

Through his marriage he becomes a bourgeois, with money, a wife, and a house. Then he has his painting. He has orders for portraits, and earns a great deal of money. He likes everything. He wants also to like the bourgeoisie and their morals, but these things seem small to him. He sees higher and farther, feels penned in by boundaries and incapable of submitting himself to convention. When he has a free moment, he returns to the wretches, and between the orders for portraits and paintings of Saskia, he takes copper and engraves two beautiful plates of a man and a woman making water.

Rembrandt rarely finds time now to devote himself to his biblical poems, to his beggars, to his turbaned easterners, to his old, old men whom he has pose for his philosophers.

Amsterdam is at the peak of its prosperity. Rembrandt has almost as many portraits to paint as Rubens and Van Dyck, portraits of the *nouveaux riches* who want to show off their wealth and power. Rembrandt paints them. He is glad to have models who are so strange, so vain, and so wealthy. For him, the entire human race is the subject for his paintings; it interests him and mollifies him. Nothing for him is more pitiable than arrogance, the pride of men or women who think that they are superior because of the wealth they possess.

He knows that they are really as poor as the lowest beggars, that their power and wealth are at the mercy of chance; but they take so much trouble to make a show, and they attach so much importance to the cut of their clothes, to the whiteness of their collars, to the emptiness of their conversation, and to their good manners, that they are very touching.

Everything entertains and interests him, but he is really happy only when he can be completely himself. He wants to paint *The Philosopher in Meditation,* to engrave a plate, *Christ Driving the Money-changers from the Temple;* to stroll; to hunt for beautiful paintings, engravings, antiquities, necklaces; to buy pretty dresses for Saskia or disguises for himself. More and more he devotes himself to his hobby of collecting. Men's dealings make him misanthropic: he shuts himself in at home and surrounds himself with all sorts of objects to make barricades behind which he lives in solitude. His house becomes the palace of a kind and melancholy tyrant. The walls are covered with his dreams: beautiful objects, beautiful fabrics are scattered everywhere; and a beautiful young wife, who is sometimes disguised as a Jewish fiancée, sometimes nude in *Susannah Coming Out of the Bath,* enlivens everything. Rembrandt lives and dreams in the middle of all that, according to the music and poetry of the Bible. Through his windows, he sees the brutal force of life in action. For him, his home is his country, his wife is his family, and all else is a ratrace.

But his wife does not understand, and she cannot tolerate his type of life. To her, Rembrandt seems to be growing further apart from her and from others.

In spite of Saskia's affection, in spite of Rembrandt's savage love, in spite of the nights that follow and atone for the wrongs of the days, Saskia is unhappy; she finds that it is not always pleasant being the wife of a famous artist.

She talks about it to her parents and to her cousin Châtelhiboux. This Hibou always knew how to maneuver, and he finds a remedy right away, a way that perhaps will fix everything and even bring him a good profit—which adds to the merit of the method. It is the custom for artists to go to Italy. Hibou, who was looking, without success, for a way to persuade Rembrandt of the usefulness of a trip to Italy, goes to his cousin. Saskia is the one who must convince Rembrandt of the necessity for this trip. She really wants to see, in the arms of her husband, this beautiful country of sun and ruins. Moreover, she hopes that, with this change of scene, Rembrandt will be distracted from his visions, will come back to her, and—her dream—will become her slave.

Rembrandt sees absolutely no necessity for this trip; he doesn't want to hear about it, and he knows that a couple of people cannot know how to achieve what he wants to do.

The ruins in the sunlight play a great part in the paintings of the Italianized painters. That is the style. He who has the whole universe within him does not want to paint ruins, to lose precious time by traveling. But his wife insists, and with some caressing, obtains what she wants from him.

It is therefore decided that they will take the trip, and Hibou will take care of the preparations.

The trip is rather long, and the stay enchanting.

He finds the Italian climate divine: that beautiful light, that ease of living, that airiness, and that good, warm, healthy sunlight about which the Nordic nostalgia always dreams. His roughness softens; his neurasthenia disappears; his sadness goes at the same time as his fervor for work. Life is too beautiful, too smooth, too luminous. Everything in this country is too beautiful and too easy for this man from the north who is used to fighting against the elements and against life.

Italy is a paradise for the man who comes from the misty north; it bathes in blue. Yet Rembrandt is too great an artist to forget completely his painting and to surrender himself entirely to his amorous fury; yet he forgets his painting, Holland, Italy, and the whole world in order to love.

Saskia is happy: her husband belongs to her, and she has to control her ardor, she has to remind him that he is an artist, and she is the one, as always, who is rational. He never thinks about anything; he wants to enjoy the sun, the pure air, to let himself live since he has found harmony. So as not to oppose his wife, he wants to paint. But he is interested only in love, in himself and her. He begins a self-portrait with a glass in his hand, Saskia on his knees, and a serving table in the foreground. It is a rather bad painting that Rembrandt does not really want to paint; and how can one paint with a woman on his knee, when one is young and in love, when one hungers only to sink his teeth into the fruits of life, and thirsts to drink in the sun, the pure air, all the wines of the earth? Living is the most beautiful painting; the rest is just appearance.

The charm is broken abruptly. Rembrandt gets a kind of indigestion from this happiness, from this dirty, eternally blue sky, the people's smiles, their sweet language; from all that Latinity that he wants to flee that very moment. Nothing stops him any more; nothing interests him more than to know when the boat will be leaving for Holland.

One beautiful gray day, a large three-masted ship returns to the port of Amsterdam with Rembrandt and Saskia aboard.

Rembrandt is in an excellent mood, and sees his city with joy. He returns to his studio, and goes back to work. Italy is too blue. He forgot his art to love only his wife, but now, in Amsterdam, he counts on catching hold of it again.

His woman, all women, he loves them; that which he loves most in them is their mystery, their veils, their spirit, their taste for spending money, their mania for adorning themselves, the poetry in them, and also their warmth, their thighs, their flesh. He loves their eyes for their inexplicability; their breasts because, along with their bellies, this is where he prefers to rest his feverish head. But he loves above all the beauty in paintings that are more beautiful to him than reality, because painting is ennobled by art, silence, and by an apparent eternity.

Saskia is a little tired; she asks a friend for the address of a midwife.

The orders continue to flow in. The rich, happy with their wealth and themselves, want to have their portraits done. The scholars are pleased with their knowledge; the writers and poets are happy with their beautiful sentences; the women are happy with their bodies and with the wealth that they elicit from them—everyone wants to be painted with the badge of his power. The sailor wants to be painted on the deck of his ship, with smoking cannon behind him and a large saber or a baton of authority in his hand. Women want to be painted with all the jewels and beautiful dresses that they earned with their beauty and competency; and if they were daring, they would have themselves painted in the bedroom, which is their battlefield. Even the virtuous people, regents of orphanages or asylums, and their wives, are so proud and pleased with their virtue that they too want to be painted.

Doctor Tulipe wants to be painted surrounded by doctors—of lesser importance, of course, and in the process of hacking up a corpse. Posterity will say, "Did you see Dr. Tulipe's portrait? Did you seé how well he can carve meat and how learned he is?" "Did you see Captain Tempête, who is fearless?" "Did you see the regents of the leper hospital? How virtuous they are; they don't even have leprosy!"

Thanks to their vanity, Rembrandt paints; and for him, Dr. Tulipe and his assistants are only models, and the blooming corpse, which he puts in the center of his painting, shows the corruption of life, the vanity of science, and the folly of pride. The captains are only actors in a tragicomedy. The regents and their wives are only poor old foolish men and poor little old women.

They are all dead and forgotten, and even their names are only used as titles for the paintings.

All his wealth, the money he earns, the sycophants who surround him, the fame and glory, disgust him. He aspires to a simple life; and he must receive many people in his home, show them his paintings, talk to them, paint them. He feels that because of his fame he has built himself a prison and he is no longer free; he feels that he who is being flattered is really the courtesan of glory. Glory is confusing his routine and violating his genius, and he throws it to the wind. He soars very high, he dominates the crowd, sees the stars and wants to reach them. He climbs on the highest clouds, stumbles, gets up, climbs still higher and farther from the earth; he still prefers light, shadows, color, lines. In the open sky above mankind, he paints. But Saskia calls him, tells him to come downstairs, and he runs. Monsieur Maurice Huygens is there for his sitting, and some great lords are paying him a visit.

He has a pressing desire to paint an *Ecce Homo* using his portraits of the bourgeoisie.

As long as Rembrandt stays on the true path, that is, works and lives as others before him, he is respected; he is serious; he can earn a living. He paints portraits as others before him have done, perhaps a little better, perhaps a little worse. He earns some money, and as the only thing he knows to do with it is to spend it, he spends it liberally. He is seen at the jewelers', he buys jewels and pearl necklaces.

He could not care less, but the bourgeois become wary, and hesitate to order portraits from a man who spends as much or more money than they. Besides, these portraits are not very famous. More and more, the things this artist paints seem strange: they are no longer real color portraits; they become bizarre; his portraits are like revenges; and it is not surprising that, because of the irregular life in the Rembrandt house, poor Saskia becomes ill and begins to waste away.

What madness it is to paint oneself dressed absurdly in turbans, feathers, jewels, old hangings; and what shame for Saskia's family are the nudes and the queer paintings on biblical subjects! Then, he receives at his house at the same time as the lords and great ladies, and with so much courtesy, all sorts of wretches, Jews (for whom he seems to have a preference), wandering minstrels, rat-poison salesmen, and ragged peasants. What a house of debauchery Rembrandt runs!

For the second time, Saskia has a miscarriage: Rembrandt does not succeed in works that require two people.

Saskia also often bores him. During the long winter evenings, when his working hours are shortened, he wants his wife to be a companion with whom he can expound on his paintings or sing folk songs or amuse himself naïvely; but Saskia is charmed by gossip; she pays calls. She goes to see the wives of the burgomasters, Madame Grotius, Madame Huygens, and Madame Anslo, and she tells little pieces of gossip of no interest because she is well bred and very proper.

But, for Rembrandt, she is unbearable at certain times. At such a time, he leaves the room without saying a word; he picks up an old pipe with a broken stem—broken in such a way that it smokes like a stove—lights this short pipe, and wanders through the countryside in the rain or snow. After an hour or two, he returns drenched but happy. He is bedewed like a tree or the earth; he has, for the moment, escaped from everything, even from his genius; and upon returning, he begins to sketch by candlelight. Wisely, Saskia goes to bed, but she does not sleep. He hears the song and movement of pots, he hears the rain fall outdoors, then he no longer hears anything, and he dreams his dreams. He forgets the warm bed, the thighs, the belly and the breasts of his wife.

During the day, there is other anguish. The visitors who come to the Rembrandt house are almost always there for him; they come to see him, to see his paintings, his etchings; they flatter him, compliment him, and in addition, there are even some compliments for Saskia. But she wants all respect. She does not speak, but her mood darkens; she is nervous, and Rembrandt does not put up with bad moods of others. He paces around the house like a troubled soul, furious with himself; and begins again a plate, *The Death of the Virgin*, but he cannot work. Then he goes toward the kitchen, finds a maid squatting to wash the floor, and lifts her skirt. Famous men are like all others. Soothed, he returns to his studio, singing.

The superintendent of police of the first district of Amsterdam is a happy man, sure of himself, and proud of his rank. His subordinates are proud of themselves and happy, but have fewer stripes. They are dangerous and stupid because they exercise some power and they carry weapons.

The superintendent's name is Coq. He knows Rembrandt, but he was pointed out as someone on whom to keep an eye: one always has friends. Coq knows nothing about painting or about pictures, but he is so self-satisfied that he wants an enormous painting to eternalize his power, his armed exploits, and his uselessness.

Rembrandt is happy as he goes to paint a whole series of wretches. He paints the representatives of order as they are; that is to say, disorderly, full of conceit and arrogance. On a large canvas, he paints a concert of colors and lines, a noisy fanfare: there is the rattling of arms; the harsh voice of the chief, who stands in the middle; the drummer on the right, the flagbearer on the left; the falsely submissive lieutenant, who pretends to listen to the chief's orders and who wants to have his position, all a fanfare of civic guards. And, ironically for all the people who have the appearance of power, a girl passes, walking a rooster with its head bowed. Superintendent Coq has his head held high.

Rembrandt paints a theatrical canvas. He well knows that it will not be his best work, but painting amuses him so much! It is such a beautiful program. He likes the theatre, its large contrivances, and its naïve symbolism. He does a large painting for the people whom he likes, and the people show their kindness by calling it a masterpiece. But the superintendent is not pleased even though he has the best position in the painting; the others are even less happy. It is too bad, but Rembrandt knows that no one is ever pleased with his portrait.

His unimportant friends say that he is really finished; moreover, he does not get good reviews. They don't understand this work; but why always search to understand?

Man's judgment is powerless when faced by one of Rembrandt's works. When one says that he or his work is good, Rembrandt says, "I don't agree with you." When another says, "It's bad," he says, "You think so, do you?" and he enjoys showing that he knows how to hurt them more. He plays with his critics like a cat plays with a mouse. Man's judgment and his unfathomable stupidity leave Rembrandt indifferent. He follows his path to the stars. Men shout and they squabble around Rembrandt. He either does not hear the arguments, or enjoys them only for a moment. Then he is caught up again by his madness. He sings his tune and hears only his own voice.

He knows that everyone is in a desperate condition, that all men thirst and hunger for the ideal. He feels that he, Rembrandt, is the rich one, the possessor of the most beautiful treasure; he knows that this is why one wants to rob him, and he draws from this conviction an excess of force to perfect, to raise higher, the monument he is in the process of working out.

Rembrandt paints for glory, he paints for love, he paints because it is the most beautiful lie. The truest and most real painting sets aside reality. A painted woman has more charm than the model who posed for the picture; reality is exalted by art. The beggars and the wretches Rembrandt paints are ugly and often repulsive, the bourgeoisie are absurd and trivial, the *nouveaux riches* are dull, but the paintings of them are masterpieces.

Saskia is sick; she is going to die. She dies in 1642, and Rembrandt is left alone with his painting, his child, and his maid. Rembrandt is thirty-six. He paints *Stormy Landscape.* Saskia's death was a storm in his life, and it is as a poet that he paints his landscapes of this period.

His painting cures him of the grief and boredom arising from his loss of Saskia. His grief does not keep him for long from the impetuous life; his boredom is a little more tenacious, but it too yields, and soon new bad habits take hold of him. Naturally, Henriette, his maid, takes care of his household and his son, gives orders for meals, and replaces the deceased in the house and in bed.

Our sentimentality makes everything of the woman one loves; one thinks he cannot go on living if the loved one disappears abruptly, but the greatest suffering is the upsetting of habits and the steps one must take in order to return to a state of tranquility. Rembrandt, who thinks this way, rushes through the steps: he dresses Henriette in his wife's clothes, undresses her, paints her; and makes love to her. This simple prostitute does it out of love, and asks for nothing else: she collaborates; helps Rembrandt; and takes care of the household.

Rembrandt, having found his lost poise, lives happily and according to the Bible, in his house on the Joodebreestraat, right in the middle of the Jewish quarter. The servants of the people in his neighborhood do not see any evil in his way of life, for woman is made for man and man for woman. But outside the Jewish quarter is Amsterdam, it's bourgeoisie with strait-laced morals, who don't understand and who, like all others elsewhere, don't admit to being incapable of understanding.

To show their superiority, they turn from Rembrandt; cause him all sorts of trouble, and bring a case against Henriette in order to make her believe that it's a crime to go to bed with a man who did not give a death notice to his sexual endeavors.

Since Rembrandt lives fully, he spends all he earns, he buys things which please him, while all the searchers of poor judgment, all the misers, all the parasites, and all the mediocrity fall upon him and hum around him. Even his parents find fault with him.

He shuts himself up in his house; his world is inside himself, and he recreates it with the magic of his genius, but he creates it as sad, deep, and human. He is a misanthrope; he sees the impossibility of happiness, but he also sees that the dream remains. And always, in each of his paintings and in each of his etchings, one sees nostalgia for paradise lost, the submission to fate, and the dream in revolt against reality. This is why, perhaps, his paintings are so thoroughly human, so sad, and so beautiful for the poor who find accomplished, on a square of painted canvas, the immensity of their aspirations.

Now Rembrandt is more and more exposed to the speculations of his creditors, but what does he care about these petty troubles? One lives only once.

He wants to live; the misers can bark like starved dogs; he doesn't even listen to them. He dreams of beauty and goodness.

Misery doesn't exist in his dreams; in Henriette's arms he finds the tenderness and warmth for which his troubled body thirsts.

A bailiff comes to demand money. Rembrandt, who knows that all—all his effort, his works, his whole life—is a magnificent gift, cannot understand that there are people who count every penny, who claim their money and force him to give it; he does not understand their right to make a claim so presumptuously, since he gives them everything. He knows that all of them are gossips and that they come to haunt him. He does good and evil things, and they are the ones who give orders; they are the ones who are arrogant because they are unimportant: he is light; they are darkness. It is for gain, desire, and meanness that they bear a grudge against his wealth. Rembrandt is exceedingly sad.

All that is perhaps only the shadow and the light of painting. He straightens up; he is again standing in his studio, light on one side and shadow on the other; a statue of light and shadow. But the day draws to an end; the sun begins to sink; shadow more and more invades the statue; there is more sadness and less joy; the clouds gather; the day is gray. Life is more formidable, the drama is greater, there is less comedy; the dream staircase becomes blurred in an opaque fog. There are several started canvases that represent old, worn-out women, weary old men, and a lavish, sad *Christ Carrying the Cross.*

Rembrandt no longer has anything: his possessions, his paintings, and his house have been sold. He lives in an inn, and has a pack of creditors always after him. He has to work for a long time in order to pay his debts. Soon the inn becomes too expensive for him. He goes to lodge in a barn; the pack follows him. He works; they take from him everything he paints in order to turn it into cash. He is alone, entirely alone: an outlaw, a pariah.

Even Henriette and Titus his son no longer follow him. Henriette, his mistress, his wife, and Titus, his son, his young cretin, found an association to exploit Rembrandt's work. Henriette is only a woman; Titus is only a young man.

His woman and his son eat his heart out.

His soul is overwhelmed by sorrow, and his body is only a plague. His love is so large that he accepts everything. He who they say is weak and incapable of managing himself—he knows human weakness, he doesn't even have pity for it. He knows that to have pity is to believe yourself superior; he submits to his love, which is larger than Christ's love; his sacrifice is even greater.

He always gives, always gives more, and always he is abandoned more. In his barn on the Canal of Roses, facing the "Labyrinthe," he bleeds from all the wounds that human foolishness gave him. He grows old alone and abandoned.

The life of an old man is a gift. Rembrandt is an old lover who worships life. His suffering and death are sadder than the life and death of Christ. Rembrandt fades into the void, into the unknown; he disappears without anyone noticing.

He dies in a corner of his barn like an abandoned dog.

1. REMBRANDT WITH CURLY HAIR
1630 (?)   *one state*

2. REMBRANDT
WITH A SOFT CAP
1634 (?)   *two states*

3. REMBRANDT WITH A FALCON
1633(?)   *four states*

*Plate numbers are from the Bartsch catalog of 1797. If a plate number is omitted
in this section, it can be found in the section "The Rejected Etchings" beginning on page 229.*

33

5. REMBRANDT
LEANING FORWARD
1630(?)   *two states*

4. REMBRANDT WITH A BROAD NOSE
1629(?)   *one state*

6. REMBRANDT
IN DARK CLOAK AND CAP
1631(?)   *three states*

34

7. REMBRANDT WEARING A SOFT CAP
1631   *six states*

8. REMBRANDT WITH LONG CURLY HAIR
1631   *seven states*

9. REMBRANDT
LEANING FORWARD,
AS IF LISTENING
1630   *one state*

10. REMBRANDT ANGRY
1630   *two states*

11. TITUS VAN RIJN, REMBRANDT'S SON
1656(?)   *one state*

12. REMBRANDT WITH FUR CAP (Oval border)
1631(?)   one state

13. REMBRANDT OPEN—MOUTHED,
AS IF SHOUTING
1630   three states

15. REMBRANDT IN CLOAK
WITH FALLING COLLAR
dated 1630, altered to 1631   five states

16. REMBRANDT
IN A HEAVY FUR CAP
1631   *two states*

17. REMBRANDT IN CAP AND SCARF (Face dark)
1633   *five states*

18. REMBRANDT WITH RAISED SABRE
1634   *two states*

19. REMBRANDT AND HIS WIFE SASKIA
1636   *six states*

20. REMBRANDT IN VELVET CAP AND PLUME
1638   *three states*

21. REMBRANDT LEANING ON A STONE SILL
1639   *three states*

22. REMBRANDT DRAWING AT A WINDOW
1648   *eight states*

23. REMBRANDT WITH PLUMED CAP AND LOWERED SABRE
1634 *four states*

24. REMBRANDT IN A FUR CAP
1630   *five states*

27. REMBRANDT WITH HIGH CURLY HAIR
1630   *one state*

26. REMBRANDT IN FLAT
CAP, WITH SHAWL
1639   *three states*

28. ADAM AND EVE
1638   *one state*

29. ABRAHAM ENTERTAINING THE ANGELS
1656   *one state*

30. ABRAHAM CASTING OUT
HAGAR AND ISHMAEL
1637   *one state*

33. ABRAHAM CARESSING ISAAC
1637(?)   *five states*

34. ABRAHAM AND ISAAC
1645   *three states*

35. ABRAHAM'S SACRIFICE
1655   *one state*

36. FOUR ILLUSTRATIONS FOR THE PIEDRA GLORIOSA
OF SAMUEL MANASSEH BEN ISRAEL
1655   *The individual plate appears in only one state.*
a. *The Image Seen by Nebuchadnezzar: four states*
b. *Daniel's Vision of the Four Beasts: three states*
c. *Jacob's Ladder: three states*
d. *David and Goliath: four states*

a.

b.

c.

d.

37. JOSEPH TELLING HIS DREAMS
1638   *five states*

38. JOSEPH'S COAT
BROUGHT TO JACOB
1633   *four states*

39. JOSEPH AND POTIPHAR'S WIFE
1634   *five states*

40. THE TRIUMPH OF MORDECAI
1641(?)   *two states*

41. DAVID AT PRAYER
1652   *three states*

42. THE BLINDNESS OF TOBIT
1651   *two states*

43. THE ANGEL DEPARTING FROM THE FAMILY OF TOBIAS
1641   *seven states*

44. THE ANGEL APPEARING TO THE SHEPHERDS
1634   *five states*

45. THE ADORATION OF THE SHEPHERDS: WITH LAMP
1654(?)   *three states*

46. THE ADORATION OF THE SHEPHERDS: A NIGHT PIECE
1652(?)   *ten states*

47. THE CIRCUMCISION IN THE STABLE
1654   *three states*

48. THE CIRCUMCISION (Small plate)
1630(?)   *one state*

49. THE PRESENTATION IN THE TEMPLE
1640(?)   six states

50. THE PRESENTATION IN THE TEMPLE: (Dark manner)
1657(?)   *one state*

51. THE PRESENTATION IN THE TEMPLE
(Small plate) 1630   *one state*

52. THE FLIGHT INTO EGYPT
(Small plate) 1633   *two states*

53. THE FLIGHT INTO EGYPT:
A NIGHT PIECE
1651   *nine states*

54. THE FLIGHT INTO EGYPT
(A sketch) 1629(?)   *six states*

55. THE FLIGHT INTO EGYPT: CROSSING A BROOK
1654   *three states*

56. THE FLIGHT INTO EGYPT
(Altered from a plate by Hercules Seghers)
two states
1653(?)

57. THE REST ON
THE FLIGHT TO EGYPT:
A NIGHT PIECE
1644(?)   *eight states*

58. THE REST ON THE FLIGHT TO EGYPT (Lightly etched)
1645   *one state*

59. THE REST ON THE FLIGHT TO EGYPT
1626(?)   *one state*

60. CHRIST BETWEEN HIS PARENTS,
RETURNING FROM THE TEMPLE
1654   *one state*

61. VIRGIN AND CHILD IN THE CLOUDS
1641   *two states*

62. THE HOLY FAMILY
1632   *two states*

63. THE VIRGIN AND CHILD WITH CAT
1654   *four states*

64. CHRIST SEATED, DISPUTING WITH THE DOCTORS
1654   *two states*

65. CHRIST DISPUTING WITH THE DOCTORS
1652   *three states*

66. CHRIST DISPUTING WITH THE DOCTORS
(Small plate) 1630   *six states*
a. first two states   b. third through sixth states

a.

b.

67. CHRIST PREACHING, (LA PETITE TOMBE)
about 1635   *three states*

68. THE TRIBUTE MONEY
about 1635   *three states*

69. CHRIST DRIVING THE MONEY—CHANGERS FROM THE TEMPLE
1635   *seven states*

75

70. CHRIST AND THE WOMAN OF SAMARIA
1657 in first state   1658 in third state
five states

71. CHRIST AND THE WOMAN OF SAMARIA: AMONG RUINS
1634   *four states*

72. THE RAISING OF LAZARUS (Small plate)
1642   *three states*

73. THE RAISING OF LAZARUS (Large plate)
1632(?)   *ten states*

74. CHRIST HEALING THE SICK
("THE HUNDRED-GUILDER PRINT")
1649(?)   *five states*

75. THE AGONY IN THE GARDEN
1663   *two states*

a.

76. CHRIST PRESENTED TO THE PEOPLE
1655   *eight states*
a. first through fifth states
b. sixth through eighth states
with arches added and much
other reworking

83

77. CHRIST BEFORE PILATE (ECCE HOMO)
1635   *four states*

78. THE THREE CROSSES
1653   *five states*

79. CHRIST CRUCIFIED BETWEEN TWO THIEVES (Oval plate)
1641(?)   *three states*

80. THE CRUCIFIXION
1635(?)   *four states*

81. I. THE DESCENT FROM THE CROSS (First plate)
1633   *(not shown—plate was a failure)*

II. THE DESCENT FROM THE CROSS (Second plate)
1633   *five states (shown here)*

82. THE DESCENT FROM THE CROSS (A sketch)
1642   *one state*

83. THE DESCENT FROM THE CROSS BY TORCHLIGHT
1654   *three states*

84. CHRIST CARRIED TO THE TOMB
1645(?)   *one state*

85. THE VIRGIN WITH THE INSTRUMENTS OF THE PASSION
1641(?)   *one state*

86. THE ENTOMBMENT
1654(?)   *five states*

87. CHRIST AT EMMAUS (Large plate)
1654   *four states*

88. CHRIST AT EMMAUS (Small plate)
    1634   *two states*

89. THE INCREDULITY OF THOMAS
    1656   *one state*

90. THE GOOD SAMARITAN
1633   *four states*

91. THE RETURN OF THE PRODIGAL SON
1636   *four states*

92. THE BEHEADING OF JOHN THE BAPTIST
1640   *four states*

94. PETER AND JOHN AT THE GATE OF THE TEMPLE
1659   *six states*

95. PETER AND JOHN AT THE GATE OF THE TEMPLE (Roughly etched)
1629(?)   *one state*

96. ST. PETER IN PENITENCE
1645   *one state*

97. THE STONING OF ST. STEPHEN
1635   *four states*

98. THE BAPTISM OF THE EUNUCH
1641   *four states*

99. THE DEATH OF THE VIRGIN
1639 *five states*

101. ST. JEROME PRAYING
1635   *four states*

100. ST. JEROME READING
1634   *two states*

102. ST. JEROME KNEELING IN PRAYER
1635   *four states*

104

103. ST. JEROME BESIDE A POLLARD WILLOW
1648   *two states*

104. ST. JEROME, READING, IN AN ITALIAN LANDSCAPE
1653   *two states*

105. ST. JEROME IN A DARK CHAMBER
1642   *five states*

107. ST. FRANCIS BENEATH A TREE, PRAYING   *one state*
1657

109. DEATH APPEARING TO A WEDDED COUPLE
1639   *one state*

110. THE PHOENIX
1658   *one state*

111. THE SHIP OF FORTUNE
1633   one state

112. MEDEA: THE MARRIAGE OF JASON AND CREÜSA
1648   *five states*

113. THE STAR OF THE KINGS: A NIGHT PIECE
1651(?)   *seven states*

114. THE LION HUNT (Large plate)
1641 *two states*

116. THE LION HUNT (Small plate, with one lion)
1629(?) *one state*

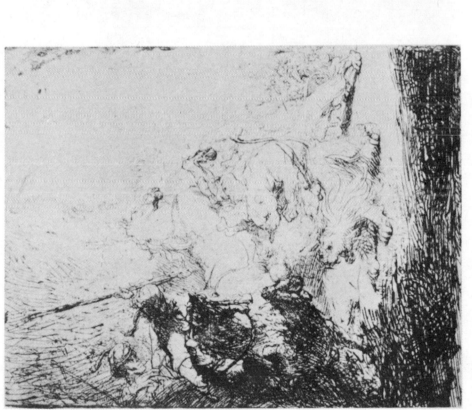

115. THE LION HUNT (Small plate, with two lions)
1641(?) *two states*

117. THE CAVALRY FIGHT
1632(?) *two states*

118. THREE ORIENTAL FIGURES
(JACOB AND LABAN?) 1641 *two states*

119. THE STROLLING MUSICIANS
1635(?)   *three states*

120. THE SPANISH GYPSY
1642(?)   *one state*

121. THE RAT KILLER
1632   *two states*

123. THE GOLDSMITH
1655   *three states*

118

124. THE PANCAKE WOMAN
1635   *six states*

125. THE GOLF PLAYER
1654   *three states*

126. JEWS IN SYNAGOGUE
1648   *seven states*

128. THE SCHOOLMASTER
1641   *three states*

129. THE QUACKSALVER
1635   *one state*

130. MAN DRAWING FROM A CAST
1641(?)   *five states*

131. PEASANT FAMILY ON THE TRAMP
1652(?)   *four states*

133. PEASANT IN A HIGH CAP,
LEANING ON A STICK
1639   *one state*

135. PEASANT WITH HIS
HANDS BEHIND HIS BACK
1631   *five states*

136. THE CARD PLAYER
1641   *four states*

138. THE BLIND FIDDLER
1631   *three states*

**139. THE TURBANED SOLDIER
ON HORSEBACK**
1632(?)   *two states*

140. POLANDER STANDING
WITH ARMS FOLDED
1635(?)   *two states*

142. A POLANDER
STANDING
WITH A STICK
1631   *one state*

141. POLANDER
LEANING ON A STICK
1632(?)   *six states*

143. OLD MAN (PROFILE)
1641(?)   *six states*

144. TWO TRAMPS:
A MAN AND A WOMAN
1634(?)   *one state*

147. OLD MAN IN MEDITATION, LEANING ON A BOOK
1645(?)   *two states*

148. STUDENT AT A TABLE BY CANDLELIGHT
1642(?)   *three states*

149. AGED MAN OF LETTERS
1627(?)   *one state*

150. BEGGAR WITH HIS
LEFT HAND EXTENDED
1631   *five states*

151. MAN IN CLOAK AND FUR CAP,
LEANING AGAINST A BANK
1630(?)   *three states*

152. THE PERSIAN
1632   *four states*

153. THE BLINDNESS OF TOBIT
(A sketch) 1629(?)   *four states*

154. TWO BEGGARS TRAMPING
1631(?)   *one state*

The same, late state

156. THE SKATER
1639(?)   *one state*

157. THE HOG
1643   *three states*

158. SLEEPING PUPPY
1640(?)   *two states*

159. THE SHELL
1650   *two states*

160. SITTING BEGGAR IN A LONG CLOAK
1630(?)   *one state*

162. BEGGAR IN A HIGH CAP,
LEANING ON A STICK
1631(?)   *one state*

163. BEGGAR
LEANING ON A STICK
1630(?)   *one state*

164. BEGGAR MAN
AND WOMAN CONVERSING
1630   *three states*

165. BEGGAR MAN AND WOMAN BEHIND A BANK
1630(?)   *seven states*

**166. BEGGAR WITH
CRIPPLED HANDS
LEANING ON A STICK**
1630(?)   *six states*

**167. BEGGAR
WITH A STICK,
WALKING**
1631   *four states*

**168. OLD BEGGAR WOMAN
WITH A GOURD**
1630(?)   *one state*

**169. BEGGAR
LEANING ON A STICK**
(Small plate) 1631(?)   *one state*

171. THE LEPER (LAZARUS KLAP)
1631   *seven states*

170. BEGGAR WOMAN
LEANING ON A STICK
1646   *six states*

172. PEASANT WITH HIS HANDS BEHIND HIM
1630(?)   *six states*

174. BEGGAR SEATED ON A BANK
1630   *two states*

173. BEGGAR WARMING HIS
HANDS AT A CHAFING DISH
1630(?)   *one state*

175. SEATED BEGGAR AND HIS DOG
1631   *one state*

176. BEGGARS RECEIVING ALMS AT DOOR
1648   *six states*

177. THE OTHER BEGGAR
1634   *one state*

178. ONE OF A PAIR
OF BEGGARS
1634   *one state*

179. BEGGAR WITH A WOODEN LEG
1630(?)   *three states*

182. TWO STUDIES OF BEGGARS
1631(?)   *one state*

188. THE FLUTE PLAYER (EULENSPIEGEL)
1642   *five states*

189. THE SLEEPING HERDSMAN
1644(?)   *one state*

190. A MAN MAKING WATER
1631   *three states*

191. A WOMAN MAKING WATER
1631   *two states*

192. THE ARTIST DRAWING FROM A MODEL
1646(?)   *two states*

144

193. NUDE MAN SEATED BEFORE A CURTAIN
1646   *two states*

194. NUDE MAN STANDING, ANOTHER SEATED
1646(?)   *seven states*

195. THE BATHERS
1651   *three states*

196. NUDE MAN SEATED ON THE GROUND
1646   *four states*

197. WOMAN SITTING HALF-DRESSED BESIDE A STOVE
1658   *eight states*

198. NAKED WOMAN SEATED ON A MOUND
1631(?)   *five states*

199. WOMAN AT THE BATH, WITH A HAT BESIDE HER
1658   *two states*

200. WOMAN BATHING HER FEET
AT A BROOK
1658   *two states*

201. DIANA AT THE BATH
1631(?)   *one state*

202. THE WOMAN WITH THE ARROW
1661   *three states*

203. JUPITER AND ANTIOPE
1659   *two states*

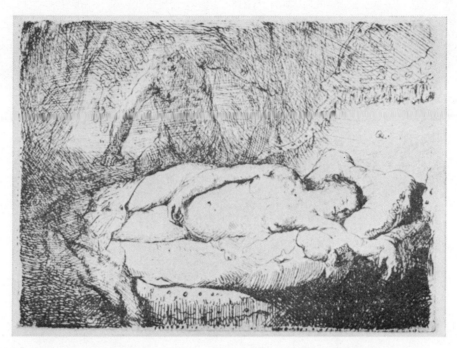

204. JUPITER AND ANTIOPE (Small plate)
1631(?)   *two states*

205. NEGRESS LYING DOWN
1658   *five states*

207. SMALL GREY LANDSCAPE
1640(?)   *one state*

208. SIX'S BRIDGE
1645   *three states*

209. THE OMVAL
1645   *four states*

210. VIEW OF AMSTERDAM
1640(?)   *one state*

211. LANDSCAPE WITH A SPORTSMAN AND DOGS
1653(?)   *two states*

212. THE THREE TREES
1643　　*two states*

213. LANDSCAPE WITH A MILKMAN
1650(?)   *two states*

217. THREE GABLED COTTAGES BESIDE A ROAD
1650   *three states*

218. LANDSCAPE WITH A SQUARE TOWER
1650   three states

219. LANDSCAPE WITH FARM BUILDINGS AND A MAN SKETCHING
1645(?)   one state

220. THE SHEPHERD AND HIS FAMILY
1644   *one state*

221. THE CANAL
1652(?)   *one state*

222. CLUMP OF TREES
1652   *two states*

223. LANDSCAPE WITH TREES, FARM BUILDINGS, AND TOWER
1650(?)   *five states*

224. LANDSCAPE WITH HAYBARN AND FLOCK OF SHEEP
1652   *two states*

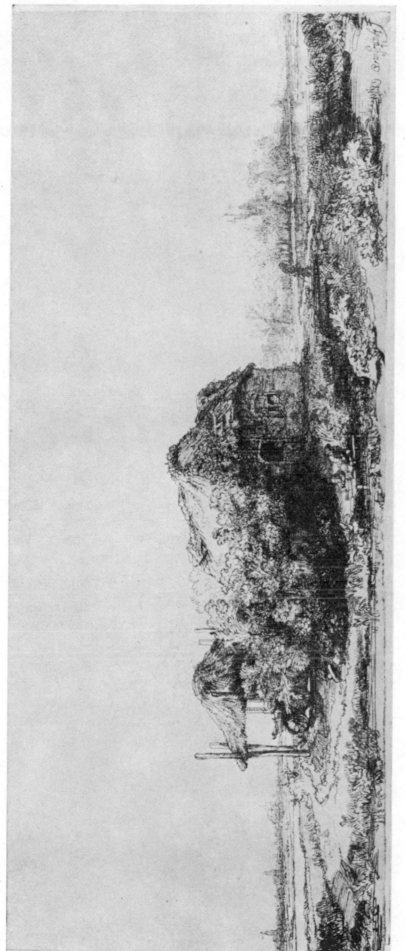

225. LANDSCAPE WITH COTTAGE AND HAYBARN
1641   *one state*

226. LANDSCAPE WITH COTTAGE AND A LARGE TREE
1641 *one state*

227. LANDSCAPE WITH AN OBELISK   *two states*
1650(?)

228. COTTAGES BESIDE A CANAL
1645(?)   *one state*

231. THE BOATHOUSE
1645   *three states*

232. COTTAGE WITH A WHITE PALING
1652   *three states*

233. THE WINDMILL
1641   *one state*

234. THE GOLDWEIGHER'S FIELD
1651   *one state*

235. THE CANAL WITH SWANS
1650   *two states*

236. CANAL WITH A LARGE BOAT
1650   *two states*

237. LANDSCAPE WITH A COW
1650(?)   *six states*

253. THE BULL
1650(?)   *one state*

257. MAN IN AN ARBOR
1642   *one state*

259. OLD MAN WITH HIS HAND ON HIS HAT
1638(?)   *five states*

260. BUST OF AN OLD BEARDED MAN
1631   *three states*

261. MAN WEARING CHAIN AND CROSS
1641   *three states*

262. OLD MAN WITH A BEARD, FUR CAP,
AND VELVET CLOAK
1632   *three states*

263. MAN WITH A BEARD AND FUR HAT
1631   *four states*

264. JAN ANTONIDES VAN DER LINDEN, PHYSICIAN
1665(?)   *seven states*

265. OLD MAN WITH A DIVIDED FUR CAP
1640   *three states*

266. JAN CORNELIS SYLVIUS
1623   *three states*

268. YOUNG MAN IN A VELVET CAP,
WITH BOOKS BESIDE HIM
1637   *one state*

269. MANASSEH BEN ISRAEL, JEWISH AUTHOR
1636   *four states*

270. FAUST IN HIS STUDY
1652(?)   *seven states*

271. CORNELIS CLAEZ ANSLO, MENNONITE PREACHER
1641 *six states*

272. CLEMENT DE JONGHE
1651   *nine states*

273. ABRAHAM FRANCEN
1657(?)   *nine states*

274. THOMAS JACOBSZ HAARING (THE OLD HAARING)
1655(?)   *one state*

275. JACOB THOMASZ HAARING (THE YOUNG HAARING)
1655   *five states*

276. JAN LUTMA, GOLDSMITH
1656   *six states*

277. JAN ASSELYN, PAINTER
1647   *six states*

278. EPHRAIM BONUS, JEWISH PHYSICIAN
1647   *one state*

279. JAN UYTENBOGAERT, ARMENIAN PREACHER
1635   *six states*

280. JAN CORNELIS SYLVIUS, PREACHER
1646   *two states*

281. JAN UYTENBOGAERT, THE GOLDWEIGHER
1639   *three states*

282. LIEVEN VAN COPPENOL (Small plate)
1658(?)   *six states*

283. LIEVEN VAN COPPENOL (Large plate)
1658(?)   *eleven states*

284. ARNOLD THOLINX

1656(?)   *two states*

285. JAN SIX
1647   *two states*

286. THE FIRST ORIENTAL HEAD
1635   *one state*

287. THE SECOND ORIENTAL HEAD
1635(?)   *two states*

288. THE THIRD ORIENTAL HEAD
1635   *one state*

289. THE FOURTH ORIENTAL HEAD
1635(?)   *three states*

290. OLD BEARDED MAN IN A FUR CAP
1635(?)   *five states*

**291. BUST OF OLD MAN WITH A
FLOWING BEARD AND WHITE SLEEVE**
1630(?)   *one state*

292. BALD MAN (REMBRANDT'S FATHER?)
1630   *two states*

**294. BALD MAN
IN PROFILE
(REMBRANDT'S FATHER)**
1630   *one state*

300. MAN CRYING OUT
1631(?)   *five states*

301. MAN CRYING OUT
*This is the same print as 300;
however, it shrank considerably,
since it was printed on parchment.
For this reason Bartsch
assigned it a separate number.*

206

302. HEAD OF
A MAN
IN A HIGH CAP
1631(?)   *two states*

303. MAN IN
A SQUARE CAP
(Right profile)
1631(?)   *two states*

305. MAN WITH A CROOKED MOUTH
1635(?)   *one state*

304. MAN WEARING A CLOSE CAP
1630   *six states*

306. BALD OLD MAN
WITH A SHORT BEARD
(?)   *two states*

307. BEARDLESS MAN
IN FUR CAP
1631   *four states*

207

310. PORTRAIT OF
A BOY: PROFILE
1641   *one state*

309. OLD MAN WITH FLOWING BEARD
1630   *one state*

311. MAN IN BROAD-BRIMMED
HAT AND RUFF
1638   *one state*

312. OLD MAN
WITH A FUR CAP
1631(?)   *two states*

313. BEARDED MAN
WEARING VELVET CAP WITH JEWEL CLASP
1637   *two states*

314. BUST OF
BEARDED OLD MAN
1631   *one state*

315. OLD MAN
WITH FLOWING BEARD
1631   *one state*

16. REMBRANDT IN A CAP,
LAUGHING
1630   *five states*

317. SNUB NOSED MAN
IN A CAP
1631   *one state*

319. REMBRANDT WITH A
CAP PULLED FORWARD
1631(?)   *seven states*

320. REMBRANDT IN A
CAP, STARING
1630   *two states*

321. REMBRANDT'S FATHER (?)
WEARING A HIGH CAP
1630   *six states*

326. GROTESQUE
PROFILE,
MAN IN A
HIGH CAP
1631(?)   *five states*

327. HEAD OF MAN
IN A FUR CAP,
CRYING OUT
1631(?)   *three states*

325. OLD MAN WITH A FLOWING BEARD
1630(?)   *one state*

333. OLD MAN
IN FUR COAT
AND HIGH CAP
Cut from the large plate 366
six states

334. BEARDED
OLD MAN
(Profile)
Cut from the large plate 366
six states

332. REMBRANDT BAREHEADED
1631(?)   *three states*

336. REMBRANDT
SCOWLING
(Octagon)
1631(?)   *one state*

337. BUST OF AN OLD MAN
WITH A WHITE BEARD

338. REMBRANDT BAREHEADED (Large plate)
1629   *one state*

340. THE GREAT JEWISH BRIDE
1635   *three states*

342. THE LITTLE JEWISH BRIDE
1638   *one state*

214

343. REMBRANDT'S MOTHER SEATED AT A TABLE
1631(?)   *three states*

345. WOMAN READING
1634   *two states*

347. SASKIA WITH PEARLS
1634   *two states*

348. REMBRANDT'S MOTHER IN ORIENTAL HEADDRESS
1631   *four states*

350. OLD WOMAN SLEEPING
1637(?)   *one state*

349. REMBRANDT'S MOTHER
WITH HAND ON CHEST
1631   *seven states*

351. REMBRANDT'S MOTHER
IN A CLOTH HEADDRESS
1632   *two states*

218

352. REMBRANDT'S MOTHER (Head only)
1628   one state

356. GIRL WITH A BASKET
1642(?)   two states

354. REMBRANDT'S MOTHER
(Head and shoulders)   1628   one state

**359. THE SICK SASKIA,
WITH WHITE HEADDRESS**
1642(?)   *one state*

362. WOMAN IN SPECTACLES READING
1642(?)   *one state*

**363. SHEET OF STUDIES: HEAD OF REMBRANDT,
BEGGARS, OTHERS**
1632(?)   *four states*

364. WOODEN PALING WITH TWO HEADS AND A HORSE
1652(?)   *one state*

365. STUDIES OF THE HEADS OF SASKIA AND OTHERS
1636   *two states*

366. SHEET OF STUDIES OF MEN'S HEADS
1631   *two trial proofs*

367. THREE HEADS OF WOMEN
1637(?)   *two states*

368. THREE HEADS OF WOMEN, ONE ASLEEP
1637   *three states*

369. SHEET OF STUDIES: WOMAN LYING ILL IN BED, OTHERS
(?)   *one state*

370. HEAD OF REMBRANDT,
BEGGAR FAMILY, OTHERS
1651(?)   *one state*

372. SHEET WITH TWO STUDIES
1642(?)   *one state*

373. SHEET OF TWO SLIGHT STUDIES,
ONE OF TWO PEASANTS
1634(?)   *one state*

374. THREE STUDIES OF OLD MEN'S HEADS
1630(?)   *one state*

THE REJECTED ETCHINGS

THE BARTSCH CATALOG of 1797 lists at least 375 etchings, whereas the Hind catalog lists fewer than 300 authentic Rembrandts. One of the most recent compilations, by K. G. Boon of the Rijksmuseum, credits only 287 to Rembrandt. We have decided to show examples of almost every plate attributed by Bartsch, but to separate the contested works into their own section.

Some of these works were evidently begun or directly inspired by Rembrandt and then completed by one of the numerous artists who studied under the master. Rembrandt actually did run an art school for some time, and one can imagine apprentices doing detail work on some idea Rembrandt no longer found challenging or interesting. It is interesting to note that the greatest number of rejected works are landscapes, for which evidently there was an appreciable market but for which Rembrandt had no special liking.

In most cases these rejected etchings were not outright forgeries, although there were certainly some of these also. They were rather an attempt to make money from the combination of a popular name with common and suitable themes. Rembrandt originally turned to etching as much for the financial possibilities as for the challenges of the medium. One must remember that mass-produced art was not nearly as available in the seventeenth century as it is today, made possible by recent advances in technology. Many middle-class burghers of Holland could afford a few etchings, but paintings were available only to the very rich. The influence of the medium on the subject matter is discussed in Frank Getlein's excellent book *The Bite of the Print,* from which the Introduction to the present volume is taken.

Rembrandt made from 50 to 500 prints from each plate. If anyone is tempted to begin collecting these etchings, let him be forewarned that modern reproduction techniques can make such excellent copies that they can fool even knowledgeable experts. Prices for Rembrandt's etchings have skyrocketed over the past several years, so it is advisable to deal with reputable galleries and check with available experts if at all possible before purchase. It is interesting to note that even the rejected etchings listed here may have a considerable market value reaching into the thousands of dollars. Whether this is because of their curiosity value, their innate artistic merit, or true confusion over attribution is difficult to say.

The comparison of rejected to accepted etchings reveals some interesting differences. The rejected work tends to be more gross and not show as fine a line or as much detail as the accepted. In the portraits and human studies that Rembrandt actually did, there seems to be a life force, an *anima,* that is missing in the others. Besides the overrepresentation of landscapes, there is one other difference in subject matter, and that is that Rembrandt dared to be different while his pupils and imitators stuck to more conventional scenes and portraits. Rembrandt would fore-shorten to emphasize, he would contrast brilliant light and black shade; the plodders, however, would turn in workmanlike jobs without that special flash of difference that denotes genius.

14. REMBRANDT
IN A SLANT FUR CAP

25. REMBRANDT
WITH BUSHY HAIR

31. ABRAHAM CASTING OUT HAGAR

32. ABRAHAM CASTING OUT HAGAR

93. THE BEHEADING OF JOHN THE BAPTIST

106. ST. JEROME KNEELING (Large plate)

108. THE HOUR OF DEATH

122. THE RAT KILLER

127. WOMAN CUTTING HER MISTRESS' NAILS

132. CUPID

134. OLD WOMAN WITH A STRING OF ONIONS

235

137. OLD MAN IN A TURBAN, STANDING WITH A STICK

145. THE ASTROLOGER

146. THE PHILOSOPHER
IN HIS CHAMBER

155. PHYSICIAN FEELING
THE PULSE OF A PATIENT

161. A TRAMP WITH WIFE AND CHILD

180. A PEASANT STANDING

181. A PEASANT WOMAN STANDING

185. SICK BEGGAR AND
OLD BEGGAR WOMAN

206. LANDSCAPE WITH COW AND SQUARE TOWER

214. VILLAGE WITH TWO GABLED COTTAGES ON A CANAL

215. LANDSCAPE WITH A COACH

216. THE TERRACE

229. CLUMP OF TREES BESIDE A DYKE ROAD

230. ORCHARD WITH A BARN

REJECTED LANDSCAPE

This group of landscapes has been almost universally rejected as not being by Rembrandt.
Probably many are by his pupils, or are imitations.
3 examples are shown below.

238. VILLAGE WITH RUINED TOWER

239. LANDSCAPE WITH A LITTLE FIGURE

242. LANDSCAPE WITH A WHITE FENCE

243. THE ANGLER IN A BOAT

244. LANDSCAPE WITH A CANAL AND CHURCH TOWER

245. LOW HOUSE ON THE BANKS OF A CANAL

246. THE WOODEN BRIDGE

247. LANDSCAPE WITH A CANAL AND PALISADE

248. THE FULL HAYBARN

249. COTTAGE WITH A SQUARE CHIMNEY

250. HOUSE WITH THREE CHIMNEYS

251. THE HAYWAIN

254. THE VILLAGE STREET

255. UNFINISHED LANDSCAPE

256. LANDSCAPE WITH A CANAL, ANGLERS, AND MILKMAN

240. CANAL WITH COTTAGES AND A BOAT

241. THE LARGE TREE

252. THE CASTLE

258. YOUNG MAN SEATED
WITH A GAME BAG

267. BAREHEADED OLD MAN WITH A BOOK

293. BALD OLD MAN IN PROFILE

295. BEARDED OLD MAN (Oval)

296. BEARDED MAN
LOOKING DOWN

297. MAN WITH
FRIZZLED BEARD

298. BUST OF A BALD MAN

308. BUST OF MAN
WITH THICK LIPS

299. HEAD OF
AN OLD MAN
IN A HIGH FUR CAP

243

318. PHILOSOPHER WITH
AN HOURGLASS

322. BUST OF A YOUNG
MAN IN A CAP

323. MAN IN A CAP
BOUND
AROUND HIS CHIN

324. A BALD MAN
IN A FUR CLOAK

328. THE PAINTER

329. YOUNG MAN
IN A BROAD-BRIMMED HAT
(Octagon)

330. YOUNG MAN
IN A BROAD-BRIMMED HAT

331. YOUNG MAN
IN A HAT WITH FEATHERS

335. SMALL HEAD
OF MAN,
FEATHER
IN HIS CAP

339. THE WHITE NEGRO

341. STUDY FOR THE GREAT JEWISH BRIDE

**344. REMBRANDT'S MOTHER IN WIDOW'S
DRESS AND BLACK GLOVES**

**346. OLD WOMAN MEDITATING
OVER BOOK**
*There is no such plate. It is a forgery
made by combining B 345 and B 352*

353. REMBRANDT'S MOTHER (Bust)

247

355. OLD WOMAN IN A BLACK VEIL

357. THE WHITE NEGRESS

358. WOMAN WITH HIGH HEADDRESS
TIED ROUND THE CHIN

360. HEAD OF AN OLD WOMAN

361. YOUNG GIRL READING

371. HEAD OF A DOG

375. SLIGHT STUDY OF WOMAN'S HEAD

376. BEGGAR IN A TALL HAT AND LONG CLOAK
(The same as 184)

377. REMBRANDT
WITH A JEWEL IN HIS CAP

BIBLIOGRAPHY

BARTSCH, ADAM. ed. *Catalogue raisonne de toutes les estampes qui forment l'oeuvre de Rembrandt et des principales pièces de ses principaux imitateurs. Composé par Gersaint, Helle, Glomy et Yver. Nouvelle édition entièrement refondue, corrigée et considerablement augmentée par Adam Bartsch.* Vienna: 1797. 8°

BIÖRKLUND, GEORGE. *Rembrandt's Etchings True and False.* New York: Museum Books, 1968.

BODE, W., AND GROOT, C. H. DE. *The Complete Work of Rembrandt* (reproduced in photogravure). 7 vols. Paris: 1897–1902. Eighth supplementary vol., containing biography and documents, 1906.

BOON, K. G. *Rembrandt, The Complete Etchings.* New York: Abrams, 1963.

BREDIUS, A. *Rembrandt: The Complete Edition of the Paintings.* Revised by H. Gerson. New York: Phaidon Publishers, 1969.

DIEHL, GASTON. *Van Dongen.* New York: Crown, 1969.

DODGSON, CAMPBELL. Annotated Chronological Catalogue of Rembrandt's Etchings: in P. G. Hamerton, *The Etchings of Rembrandt.* London: 1904.

GETLEIN, FRANK. *The Bite of the Print.* New York: Potter, 1963.

HAAK, BOB. *Rembrandt: His Life, His Work, His Time.* Translated from the Dutch by Elizabeth Willems-Treeman. New York: Harry N. Abrams, 1969.

HAMERTON, PHILIP GILBERT. *The Etchings of Rembrandt.* New York: Macmillan, 1894.

HIND, ARTHUR M. *A Catalogue of Rembrandt's Etchings.* New York: Da Capo Reprint, 1967.

———. *Rembrandt.* Cambridge: Harvard University Press, 1932.

KNUTTEL, GERHARDUS. *Rembrandt Etchings.* The Hague: Boucher, 1961.

METROPOLITAN MUSEUM OF ART. *The Life of Christ in Rembrandt's Etchings.* New York: The Museum Press, 1942.

MUNZ, LUDWIG. *Rembrandt Etchings.* London: Phaidon, 1952.

NOWELL-USTICKE, G. W. *Rembrandt's Etchings: States and Values.* Narbeth, Pa.: Livingston, 1967.

ROSENBERG, JAKOB. *Rembrandt.* Cambridge: Harvard University Press, 1948.

SCHILD, CONSTANCE. *The Complete Etchings of Rembrandt.* New York: Arden, 1937.

VAN DYKE, J. C. *The Rembrandt Drawings and Etchings with Critical Reassignments to Pupils and Followers.* New York: Scribner's, 1927.

WHITE, CHRISTOPHER. *Rembrandt as an Etcher: A Study of the Artist at Work.* University Park: The Pennsylvania State University Press, 1969.